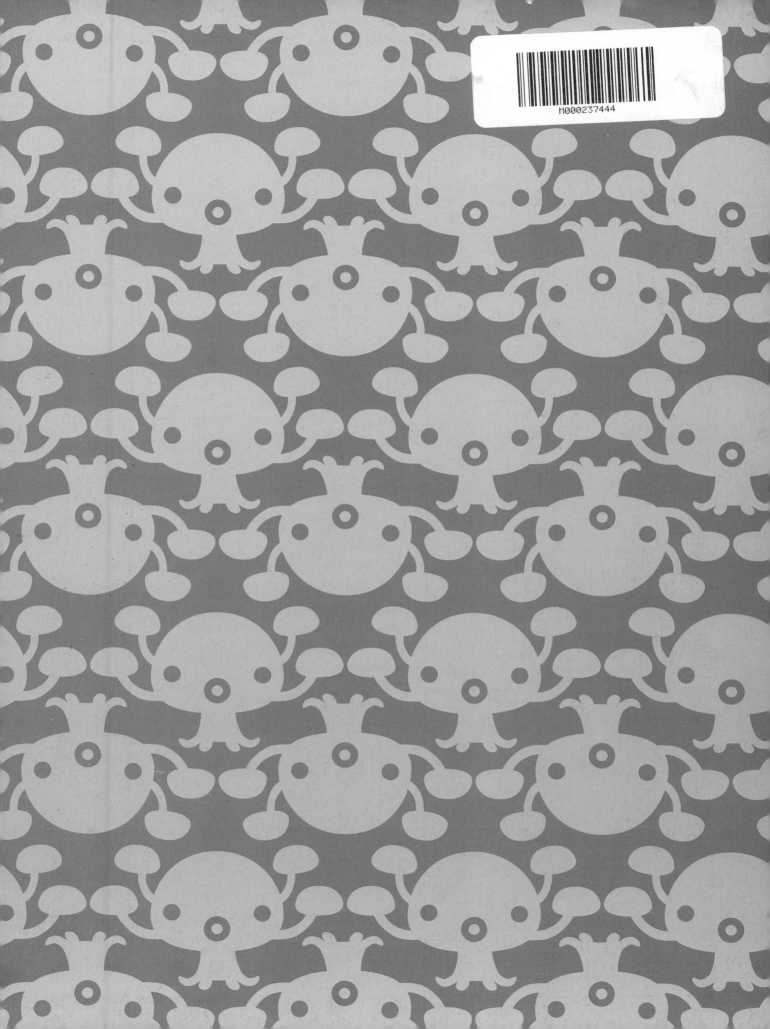

THIS OCTONAUTS ANNUAL BELONGS TO

....

OCTONAUTS™

ANNUAL 2013

EGMONT
We bring stories to life

First published in Great Britain in 2012
by Egmont UK Limited, 239 Kensington High Street, London W8 6SA

Written by Leah James. Designed by Andrea Pollock.
Special thanks to Karen and Seth Weston for the Make Your Own Peso activity.

OCTONAUTS™ OCTOPOD™ Meomi Design Inc. OCTONAUTS Copyright © (2012) Vampire Squid Productions Ltd,
a member of the Silvergate Media group of companies. All rights reserved.

ISBN 978 1 4052 6339 9
51548/1
Printed in Italy

Adult supervision is recommended when glue, paint, scissors and other sharp points are in-use.

CONTENTS

WELCOME TO THE OCTOPOD!..............................7

THE A TO Z OF THE OCTONAUTS.............................8

WELCOME TO THE SUNLIGHT ZONE!.....................16

STORY: THE OCTONAUTS AND THE GIANT JELLY...................18

CREATURE REPORT: GIANT COMB JELLY.....................26

OCTOSUMS...28

BARNACLES VS KWAZII....................................29

OCTOPOD DRAWING......................................30

DASHI MATCH...31

WELCOME TO THE TWILIGHT ZONE!.....................32

STORY: THE OCTONAUTS AND THE COOKIECUTTER SHARKS...........34

CREATURE REPORT: COOKIECUTTER SHARK.................42

HOW MANY VEGIMALS?...................................44

BARNACLES TO THE OCTOPOD!...........................45

FASCINATING FACT!.....................................46

WHO SAID THAT?..47

WELCOME TO THE MIDNIGHT ZONE!.....................48

STORY: THE OCTONAUTS AND THE SLIME EELS..................50

CREATURE REPORT: SLIME EEL...........................58

MIDNIGHT SPOT...60

BARNACLES' ADVENTURE.................................62

ON THE LOOKOUT!......................................63

MAKE YOUR OWN PESO.................................64

RACE AGAINST TIME!...................................66

ANSWERS...68

WELCOME TO THE OCTOPOD!

Join the Octonauts and help them to
EXPLORE, RESCUE, PROTECT!

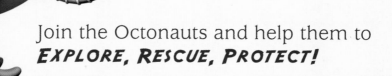

BARNACLES, KWAZII AND PESO ARE READY TO GO!
Colour in their pictures as neatly as you can.

Lots of the things below are hidden in this annual.
Count them up and write how many there are in each circle.

Answers on page 68.

WELCOME TO THE WORLD OF THE OCTONAUTS!

Here's the A to Z of Captain Barnacles and his crew.
Write over the dotty letters as you go.

 is for **alert**

"Sound the Octoalert!" When Barnacles hits the alert button, the Octonauts spring into action!

 is for **Barnacles**

Captain Barnacles is a polar bear, and he grew up in the icy Arctic.

Barnacles is the strongest Octonaut!

 is for **cook**

Tunip is the Octopod's cook. All of the Octonauts love his tasty kelp cakes!

Tunip is the leader of the Vegimals.

Dd is for Dashi

Dashi is the official Octonaut photographer.

Dashi is a girly girl – almost everything in her bedroom is pink!

Ee is for explore

The Octonauts love to explore new underwater worlds. Explore, Rescue, Protect!

Ff is for finder

Each sub has a Gup-finder that allows it to be tracked by the Octopod.

is for **GUP-C**

GUP-C is a tug-sub with enough power to tow an Orca.

H h **is for** **helmet**

All of the Octonauts have a watertight helmet that comes out of their collars at the touch of a paw.

I i **is for** **Inkling**

Professor Inkling Octopus can read eight books at once – one in each tentacle!

Inkling is the founder of the Octonauts.

J j  **is for** **jellyfish**

Jellyfish are found in every ocean, from the sunlight to the midnight zones.

K k is for Kwazii

Kwazii is Barnacles' right-hand man and a cat with a mysterious pirate past.

Kwazii has two good eyes – he only wears an eye patch because he likes it!

L l is for lab

The lab is where you will find Shellington as he studies new undersea life.

M m is for monitor

Every room in the Octopod, and every Gup, has a monitor. This means that the Octonauts can stay in touch all the time.

N n is for net

The Octonauts use nets to scoop up endangered or poorly creatures.

O o is for **Octopod**

The Octopod is the mobile home base of the Octonauts.

The Octopod's engine is powered by bubbles!

P p is for **Peso**

Peso Penguin is the Octonauts' very brave medic – he's always ready to help creatures in need.

Peso can play the xylophone!

Q q is for **quarters**

'Quarters' is the name for rooms on a ship. Each Octonaut has their own quarters.

Rr is for **reef**

The colourful coral reef is in the Sunlight Zone, and is home to giant clams, humuhumu fish and manta rays.

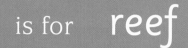

Ss is for **Shellington**

Shellington Sea Otter is a field researcher and the go-to Octonaut for sea creature facts.

Shellington loves everything about clams – he even has clam toothpaste!

Tt is for **Tweak**

Engineer Tweak Bunny designed and built all of the Gups.

Tweak keeps carrots in her toolbox!

U u is for undersea ambulance

Gup-E turns into an ambulance with a flashing siren when there's a fishy first-aid emergency.

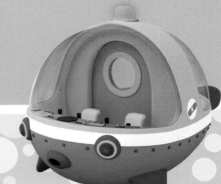

V v is for Vegimals

CHEEPA CHEEPA!

Shellington discovered the Vegimals – the first half-plant, half-animal life form!

Vegimals speak Vegimalese!

W w is for water tank

Peso has a water tank in his Infirmary, ready for any poorly water-breathing sea creatures.

X x is for GUP-X

GUP-X has the X factor! It is the toughest Gup ever and divides into 3 smaller Gups – the octo-glider, octo-tank and octo-ski.

Y y is for Yeow!

Kwazii loves to say this when he's ready to pounce into action.

YEOW!

Z z is for zone

Oceans are made up of 3 different zones – Sunlight, Twilight and Midnight. The Octonauts are ready to explore, rescue and protect in all of them!

READ ON TO LEARN MORE ABOUT THE ZONES!

WELCOME TO THE

Most sea creatures live in the Sunlight Zone. This zone is near the surface of the ocean, and is warmed by the sun in the daytime. Some creatures living in this zone are light on the bottom and dark on top. This means that when predators look up from below, or down from above, they can't see the creatures – their dark tummies and light backs camouflage them!

OCTOFACT:
A predator is an animal or sea creature that eats other animals or creatures.

OCTOFACT:
Camouflage is when the colour or shape of an animal lets it hide in the things around it.

WHO LIVES HERE?

CARRIER CRABS
Carrier crabs sometimes have spiky sea urchins living on their backs! The urchin's spikes help to keep the crab safe, and the crab helps his urchin friend to find food.

Can you draw an urchin on the crab's back? They look like this:

COMBTOOTH BLENNY
Some combtooth blennies can walk on land by using their long fins like feet! They are very colourful – colour this one in using red, blue and yellow.

SUNLIGHT ZONE!

Lots of creatures living in the Sunlight Zone have names beginning with an S. Can you find them all in this word grid?

One of the Octonauts is hiding in the grid too – can you find who it is?

TIP: this brave Octonaut is always ready to help any hurt sea creature!

S	E	A	H	O	R	S	E	S
A	C	F	G	S	I	H	K	T
I	U	S	P	A	M	R	L	A
L	S	H	A	R	K	I	P	R
F	V	S	P	D	Y	M	O	F
I	B	D	E	I	G	P	J	I
S	E	A	S	N	A	I	L	S
H	S	R	O	E	S	H	E	H
B	L	I	M	T	E	E	L	T

SEA HORSE   STARFISH   SEA SNAIL
SHARK   SHRIMP   SARDINE
SAILFISH

_____

Write your answer here.

17

"Octonauts, let's split up so we can discover more new and interesting creatures!" announced Captain Barnacles.

Barnacles was in GUP-A with Shellington and Dashi. Peso and Kwazii were behind them, mission-ready in GUP-E.

"Aye aye, Captain!" said Kwazii. **WHOOSH!** GUP-E zoomed off … straight towards a giant pink blob!

"Shiver me whiskers! What are you?" growled Kwazii, as the Gup came to a stop. "Beast or balloon?"

"It's a giant comb jelly!" said Shellington over the radio. "Like a jellyfish, but they don't sting. Luckily for Kwazii."

Daredevil Kwazii was outside GUP-E, having a closer look at the jelly.

"Peso, quick!" he said into his helmet communicator. "This jelly is hurt! One of his combs looks broken."

"I'm on my way!" said Peso. He grabbed his medical kit and rushed outside. He put his kit down and rubbed a waterproof cream on the jelly's comb to help it get better.

"Hurt!" squealed the jelly, wiggling his combs.

"All finished," said Peso. "I'll just put the cream back in my medical kit …"

But when Peso reached down, his kit had gone! He looked up and saw it floating around in the jelly's belly. **OH NO!** Peso couldn't cure any poorly creatures without his medicines – he had to get the kit back! He reached one flipper inside the jelly's belly … but **POP!** the jelly swallowed Peso up too!

GUP-A arrived at the scene of the emergency. Barnacles, Shellington and Dashi swam out to join Kwazii and Peso.

"**YEOW!**" bellowed Kwazii at the jelly. "Let him go, you big-bellied beast!"

"Go, go!" giggled the jelly.

"No! No go, go!" cried Peso. He was trying to be brave, but was just a little bit worried about what the jelly was planning to do …

"Octonauts!" announced Barnacles. "We need to get Peso out!"

"It's going to be tricky," explained Shellington. "The jelly is see-through, but has lots of layers of clear skin around a tummy full of water."

"And Peso …" Barnacles started.

But just then, they heard Peso shout, "No, please stop!"

The Octonauts turned to look – the jelly had started to swim off, with Peso in his belly!

"Kwazii, Dashi, get the GUP-A," ordered Barnacles. "Shellington, let's go after him!"

Barnacles and Shellington swam as fast as they could, but they couldn't catch up with Peso and the giant jelly.

"Sound the Octoalert!" announced Barnacles. "Octonauts – to the Gups!"

Barnacles radioed Tweak. "Peso is stuck inside a comb jelly, and the jelly is being swept away by the current! Stand by – we might need your help."

Meanwhile, the jelly was still on the go, go! He bounced along, with Peso wobbling around and around in his big see-through belly.

"Whoa!" cried the brave medic. "Watch out, jelly, we're going to crash!"

"Going to splash!" giggled the jelly. He bounced onto the sea floor, **BOING!** and **POP!** Peso shot out of the jelly's belly … right onto the nose of a great white shark! **BUMP!**

OCTOFACT!
Great white sharks eat everything, even other sharks!

21

"Oh no! Help!" cried Peso. He tried to
call his friends but he was too far away and
his radio only crackled. Peso looked behind him. The big, scary shark was
coming closer and closer … "What would Barnacles do?" thought Peso.

"Peso! Inside jelly's belly!" squealed the pink creature and **POP!** Peso
was back in his new friend's tummy. The jelly and Peso bounced away,
straight into a tunnel in the ocean floor, where the shark couldn't get them.
WHOOSH! They fell down and down, and out the other end of the tunnel.

Peso tried his radio again. "Hello, Octonauts? Can you hear me? Hello?"

But there was no answer. Now Peso really was lost. It was very dark, too.
He gulped, and tried to not to think
of the great white shark with the
big sharp teeth …

OCTOFACT:

Tunnels in the seabed
can form when volcanoes
erupt.

Meanwhile, Captain Barnacles had realised that Peso was out of radio contact. He asked Dashi to try and locate their brave medic.

"It could take months!" growled Kwazii. He was very worried.

But clever Dashi had already found a way to turn GUP-A's Gup-finder map into a Peso-finder.

"I can use the map to find Peso's radio!" said Dashi. "Look, there he is!" Peso's radio popped up on the screen as a flashing orange dot.

"It looks like he's fallen down some sort of tunnel," said Barnacles. "He's at the bottom now, near the Twilight Zone!"

"*YEOW!* Let's go and rescue Peso from that scallywag!" bellowed Kwazii. "Full speed ahead ... that is, when you say so, Captain!"

23

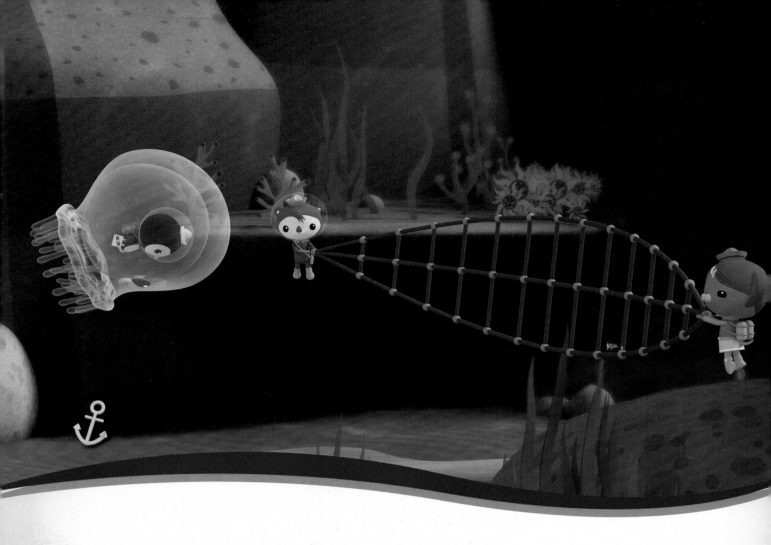

Back at the tunnel, Peso was starting to worry. At least he felt a little bit safer inside jelly's belly than outside in the dark, alone …

Jelly wanted to play – he was having a lovely time with his new penguin pal! But Peso wasn't in the mood to play – he wanted to get home.

Just then, GUP-A zoomed into sight. Peso was found, hooray! Now the Octonauts just had to get him out of his jelly-belly prison …

Dashi and Shellington swam towards Peso and the jelly, ready to put their plan into action. As the jelly started to swim off once again, they each took one end of a huge net. The jelly swam into it, **BOING!** and **POP!** out came Peso, free at last.

"Fun, fun!" said the jelly, as Peso checked the injured comb.

"Well, I guess it was quite fun," said Peso. "And your comb is better now, so no harm done."

Dashi took out her camera. "Let's take a picture of your new friend, Peso," she said. "Although it's a bit dark down here …"

Suddenly, the jelly lit up like a big pink lamp!

"Jumpin' jellyfish!" said Shellington. "Oh, I mean jumpin' comb jelly! I've never seen anything like it!"

"He's like a floating light show!" said Kwazii.

"Good work, Peso!" said Captain Barnacles. "You found a new creature *and* a new friend. Mission accomplished!"

THE END

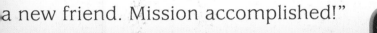

OCTOFACT:

The giant comb jelly can glow in a rainbow of colours because its combs reflect light.

CREATURE REPORT:

Now you've read a story about the giant comb jelly, read this report and learn the facts!

This jelly doesn't sting like a jellyfish does.

It has layers of skin around a belly filled with water.

A giant comb jelly will eat anything, from plankton to fish eggs.

Its body has little tails that glow in a rainbow of colours!

The tails help the jelly to swim, and to capture and eat food.

PLANKTON IS THE FLOATING ANIMAL AND PLANT LIFE IN THE SEA WATER.

Now you know all about the giant comb jelly, can you write its name?

giant comb jelly

GIANT COMB JELLY

The giant comb jelly lives in the Sunlight Zone, with sea horses and North American eels.

Can you draw one sea horse and one eel, by copying the pictures? It will be easy if you do it square by square. When you've finished, colour them in!

OCTOSUMS

There are lots of creatures to keep track of in the Sunlight Zone.

Have a go at these OctoSums to see how many you can count!

 and  makes

OCTOFACT: Anemones can make copies of themselves by splitting down the middle.

Circle all the reef lobsters. How many are there?

Now count up the giant clams:

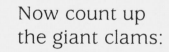

How many creatures are there when you add the lobsters and clams together?

Make these groups of kelp fish the same by drawing some more in the second circle.

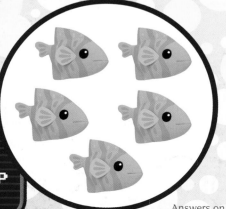 

OCTOFACT: Kelp fish hide and hunt in kelp forests.

Answers on page 68.

BARNACLES VS KWAZII

Barnacles in GUP-A and Kwazii in GUP-B are racing around the Sunlight Zone!

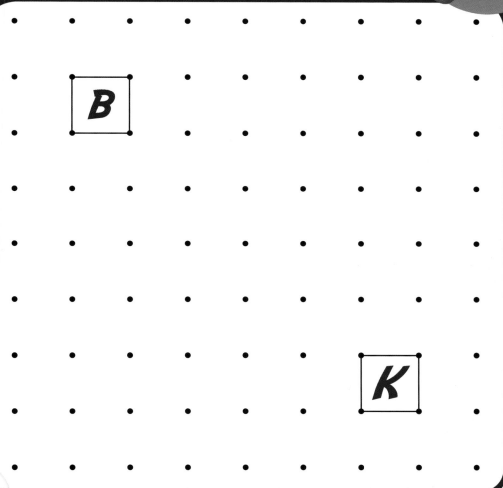

Play this game with a friend. One of you can be Barnacles and the other Kwazii. Take it in turns to draw a line connecting any two dots – no diagonals allowed! Try to make a four-sided square. The player who finishes the square puts their initial inside it. (B if you're Barnacles and K if you're Kwazii!)

When there are no more dots left, count up the letters. The player with the most boxes wins the game!

OCTOPOD DRAWING

The Octopod has just landed in the Sunlight Zone. Can you draw over the lines to complete the picture? Then colour it in.

Why don't you draw some Sunlight Zone creatures in the sea around the Octopod?

OCTOFACT:

ALL the areas in the Octopod are connected by chutes, so the Octonauts can move around quickly.

DASHI MATCH

Only 2 of these pictures of Dashi recording life in the Sunlight Zone are the same. Can you see which two they are? Draw a circle around them.

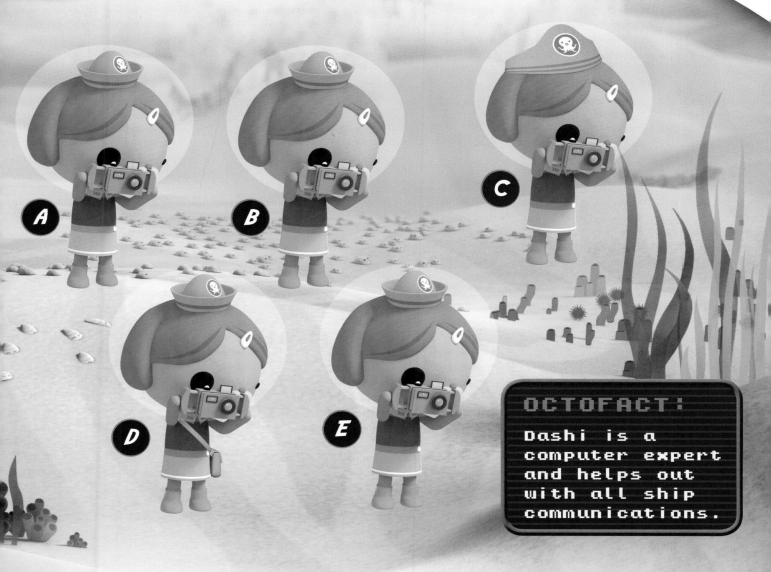

OCTOFACT:

Dashi is a computer expert and helps out with all ship communications.

Dashi is a photographer. She loves to take photos of sealife, as well as of the other Octonauts. Write over the letters to help you learn how to spell this long word:

photographer

Answer on page 68.

WELCOME TO THE

The Twilight Zone is the middle layer of the ocean. The sunlight only just reaches this far, so the water is dark blue and very cold. Lots of the sea creatures that live in the Twilight Zone have big eyes to help them see in the dark and large jaws to help them catch food.

OCTOFACT:
Some Twilight Zone creatures can make their own light.

OCTOFACT:
There are no plants in this zone because plants need lots of sunlight to grow.

WHO LIVES HERE?

DOGFISH
Dogfish are sharks, not fish! Some have spiny backs to protect them from predators. They all eat squid and octopus.

Can you draw an octopus for this dogfish to catch? TIP: they have 8 tentacles.

SPOOKFISH
Spookfish have googly eyes and see-through heads! They live at the very top of the Twilight Zone.

Colour this crazy spookfish in. TIP: they are usually bright green!

TWILIGHT ZONE!

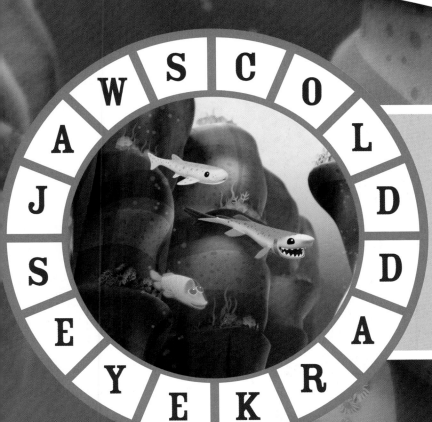

TWILIGHT WHEEL

Following the letters clockwise, which four words about the Twilight Zone and its creatures can you find in this wheel?

GUP PUZZLE

This Gup is using its lantern to explore the Twilight Zone. Can you unscramble the picture to find out which Gup this is? Tip: This Gup is usually driven by Barnacles.

THE OCTONAUTS AND THE

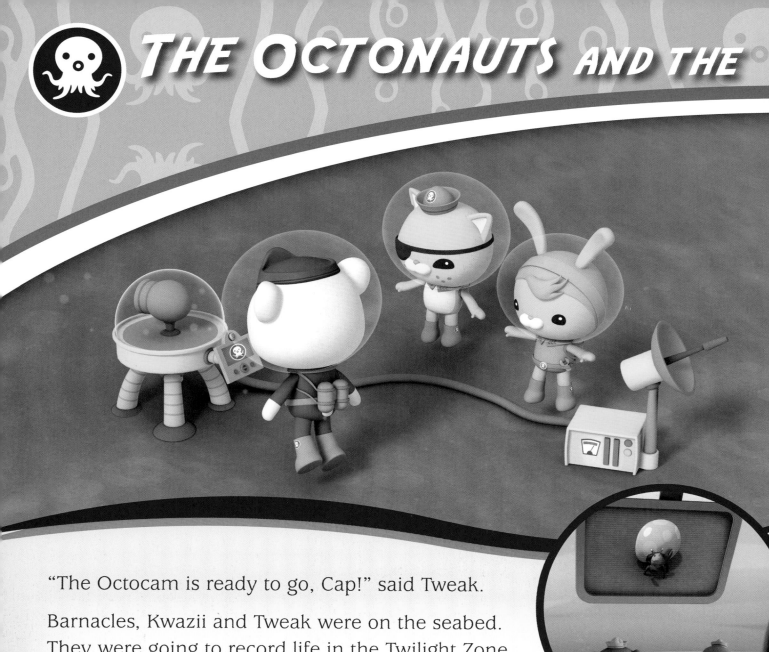

"The Octocam is ready to go, Cap!" said Tweak.

Barnacles, Kwazii and Tweak were on the seabed. They were going to record life in the Twilight Zone.

Shellington called them on the radio. "The image of the hermit crab is coming through nice and clear!"

"Excellent work, Octonauts," said Barnacles. "Let's head back to the Octopod!"

The three Octonauts jumped into GUP-A. But on their way to the Octopod, they heard a strange sound. **CRUNCH!**

"That's coming from outside the Gup!" said Kwazii. **CRUNCH!** "But I can only see those tiny skinny black fishies …" **CRUNCH!**

"GUP-A probably just needs a check-up," said Tweak. "I'll take a look when we get home."

Back on-board the Octopod,
Shellington was watching images from the
Octocam on a monitor. Suddenly, the screen went blank.

"Captain, something's wrong with the Octocam!" he said.

"Hmmm," wondered Barnacles. "It was OK when we left it behind
on the ocean floor …"

Just then, Tweak's face popped up on the monitor.

"Cap, can ya c'mon down here? There's something you've gotta see
to believe!"

Down in the launch bay, Tweak showed Barnacles three round holes in the
back of the GUP-A. And stuck in one of them was a set of sharp, pointy teeth!

"Something smells fishy here," bellowed Barnacles.
"We need to find out what's broken the Octocam and
made holes in the GUP-A!"

"Cap," said Tweak, "I'll have those holes in the Gup fixed up faster
than you can say 'buncha munchy, *crrrunchy* carrots'!"

Barnacles sounded the Octoalert, and called the Octonauts to the
launch bay.

"Shellington, find out whose teeth these are!"

"Peso, Kwazii – you're with me in GUP-A!
This is a mystery and we've got to solve it!"

GUP-A was fixed and ready to go, so the
three Octonauts jumped in and shot
down to the seabed.

Shellington was right – the Octocam had stopped working.

"Aha, here's why the camera is broken!" said Barnacles. "There are three holes in this end of the rubber cable."

Peso gasped. "Just like the ones in the Gup!"

"Hmm, I wonder who is biting our equipment?" said Barnacles. "There's nothing around except for those skinny black fish …"

"**YEOW!** I think it's none other than the Tri-Toothed Terror!" cried Kwazii. "A giant sea monster with three, huge, sharp teeth!"

The Octonauts swam around to investigate, and Peso found another set of teeth! But when Barnacles and Kwazii came to look, the teeth had disappeared …

Just as the Octonauts were wondering where the teeth had gone, they heard a deep rumbling sound. They swam towards it. It was a huge blue whale with the giggles!

"**OOH HAHAHA!** Something's tickling my blubber," boomed the whale to the Octonauts. "**OOH HAHAHA!** Can you find out who it is and stop them please? It's down by my tail now! **OOH HAHAHA!**"

Barnacles went to have a look and found three holes near the whale's tail. And then Peso found three more under the whale's chin!

"Aha! We've seen these marks before," Barnacles told the whale. "Don't worry, the Octonauts will soon find the troublemaker and stop him!"

OCTOFACT:
Blubber is the name for a whale's fat.

OCTOFACT:
Blue whales eat krill, which is like a tiny shrimp.

Meanwhile, Shellington was still flicking through the creature records on the computer. He was trying to find out which creature the teeth belonged to.

"Too big, too small ... Hey, that's it!" he said suddenly.

He radioed the team on the ocean floor. "Captain, the teeth belong to a cookiecutter shark! They dig their teeth into a whale's blubber, or anything soft, like rubber. They leave round holes, in the same way that a cookiecutter leaves a shape in dough!"

"Well done, Shellington!" said Barnacles. "Now we need to stop these rubber-blubber lovers from biting our stuff! But first we need to catch them ..."

Captain Barnacles told the Octonauts his big plan. "Octonauts, let's do this!"

A little later, the Octonauts were mission-ready. Tweak had arrived at the Octocam site in GUP-C, towing a big rubber whale balloon. Barnacles' plan was to trick the cookiecutter sharks into thinking the balloon was a real whale, and then catch them in the act of biting holes!

"Right," said Barnacles. "Let's put the balloon near the Octocam. Now, everybody hide!"

The Octonauts swam off in different directions to lie in wait for the sharks. They waited. And they waited. And they waited. Until, finally, **PSSSSSSST!** The three sharks had bitten holes in the giant balloon and the air was coming out!

"Stop there, you nasty nibblers!" growled Kwazii.

"We want to know why you broke our camera!" demanded Captain Barnacles.

"We're very sorry!" said one of the sharks. "We thought your equipment was food so we took a nibble!"

"But how did you keep hiding from us?" asked Peso. "Well," said the second shark, "our bellies glow so we blend in with the water. That means when you see us from below we look like little black fish."

"Aha! So I did see you!" said Barnacles. He had seen the little black fish behind the GUP-A, at the Octocam site *and* by the blue whale!

"And why did the teeth disappear?" asked Peso.

"They disappeared because I ate them!" said the third shark. "We eat our teeth when they fall out because they are very good for us."

The sharks promised not to nibble on any more equipment but they were still feeling hungry for a snack.

Barnacles was happy to give them one of Tunip's fish biscuits.

"This is way better than rubber," said the first shark, with his mouth full!

THE END

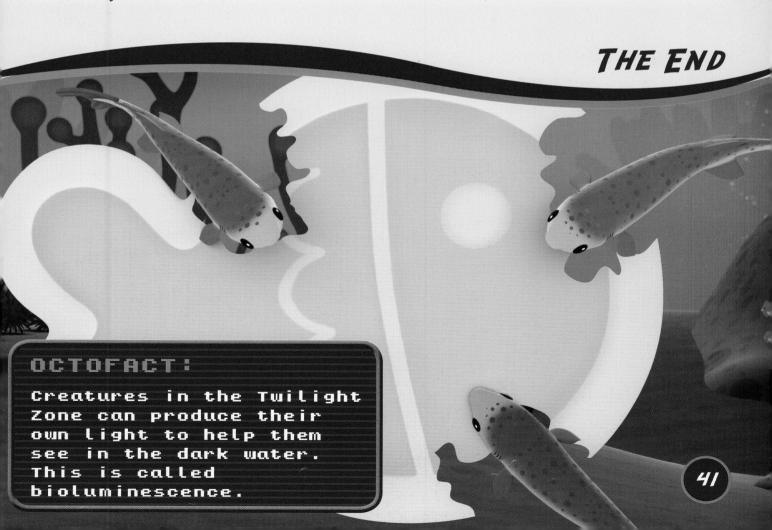

OCTOFACT:
Creatures in the Twilight Zone can produce their own light to help them see in the dark water. This is called bioluminescence.

41

CREATURE REPORT:

Now you've read a story about the cookiecutter shark, read this report and learn the facts!

Their bellies are always lighter than their backs.

This creature will bite anything that looks like blubber, leaving a hole – just like a cookiecutter!

The belly glows, helping the shark to hide from predators.

It has large eyes to help it see in the dark water.

This shark eats its own teeth when they fall out.

SHARKS LIKE THIS ONE TRAVEL IN SCHOOLS. A SCHOOL IS A GROUP OF FISH THAT SWIM AND LOOK FOR FOOD TOGETHER.

Now you know all about the cookiecutter shark, can you write its name?

cookiecutter

COOKIECUTTER SHARK

The cookiecutter shark lives in the Twilight Zone with giant spider crabs, giant squid and funny-looking blobfish.

Can you match the creatures with their shadows?

A GIANT SPIDER CRAB

B

C BLOBFISH

GIANT SQUID

1

2

3

Write your answers in the boxes.

A MATCHES SHADOW		B MATCHES SHADOW		C MATCHES SHADOW	

Answers on page 68.

OCTOFACT!
Blobfish float in one place, waiting for their food to arrive.

HOW MANY VEGIMALS?

The Octonauts are on a mission in the Twilight Zone, so the Vegimals are cooking clam-flavoured kelp cakes for when the team gets home.

How many Vegimals can you count?

How many kelp cakes can you see?

OCTOFACT:

The Vegimals always work together, just like a school of fish.

OCTOFACT:

Kelp is a type of seaweed.

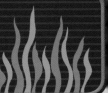

BARNACLES TO THE OCTOPOD!

Barnacles has been out exploring in the GUP-A. He is on his way home, but it's night-time and the Gup's lantern has broken!

Can you help him through the dark Twilight Zone to the Octopod? The glowing bellies of the lanternsharks can help to light the way. Watch out for the giant squids that might squirt ink at Barnacles!

Answers on page 68.

FASCINATING FACT!

Professor Inkling knows a fascinating fact about a special Twilight Zone creature. You can find out what it is by crossing out the following from the grid below:

OCTONAUTS   COLOURS   GUPS

IF	KWAZII	A	SEA
STAR	BLUE	GUP-A	LOSES
GUP-F	AN	ARM	RED
IT	SHELLINGTON	GUP-C	GROWS
A	NEW	GREEN	ONE

OCTOFACT!
Professor Inkling is
the oldest Octonaut.

Answer on page 68.

WHO SAID THAT?

Draw a line to match the Octonauts to their favourite sayings.

A   **B**   **C**   **D**   **E**

CHEEPA! CHEEPA! **1**

JUMPIN' JELLYFISH! **2**

SAY SEAWEED! **3**

I'LL BE A SEA MONKEY'S UNCLE! **4**

FLAPPITY FLIPPERS! **5**

Kwazii likes to shout "Yeow!" How many times does "yeow" appear in this wordsquare?

Write your answer here:

A	D	E	P	S
Y	E	O	W	R
E	B	I	L	N
O	C	F	H	K
W	Y	E	O	W

WELCOME TO THE

The Midnight Zone is at the bottom of the ocean.
It is so deep down that no sunlight reaches there.
The zone is completely dark and freezing cold.
The Octonauts often wear deep-sea diving suits on missions
to the Midnight Zone.

OCTOFACT:
Deep-sea diving suits let the diver breathe normally underwater.

OCTOFACT:
There is no light in this zone so some of the creatures don't have eyes.

WHO LIVES HERE?

STARFISH
Starfish don't have brains! But they can have as many as 24 arms.

Can you draw a starfish next to this one? How many arms will yours have?

ANGLER FISH
This fish has a light sticking out of its head! The light attracts other fish, and then the angler fish eats them!

Colour in the angler fish.

MIDNIGHT ZONE!

VAMPIRE SQUID

The vampire squid has a spiky web between its tentacles that looks like a cape. It uses its cape to hide from predators.

Look carefully at this page and answer the questions below. The letters in the blue boxes will spell out something about Kwazii's past!

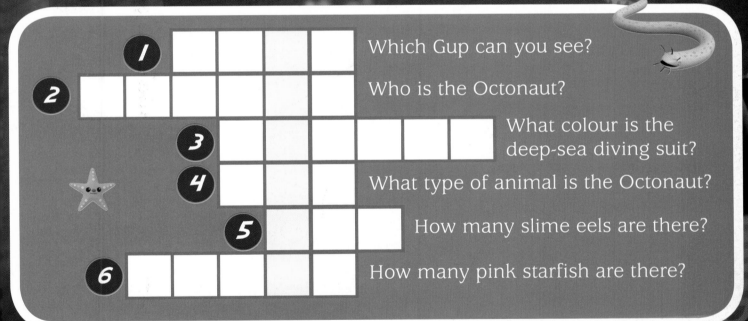

1. Which Gup can you see?
2. Who is the Octonaut?
3. What colour is the deep-sea diving suit?
4. What type of animal is the Octonaut?
5. How many slime eels are there?
6. How many pink starfish are there?

49

Answers on page 68.

THE OCTONAUTS

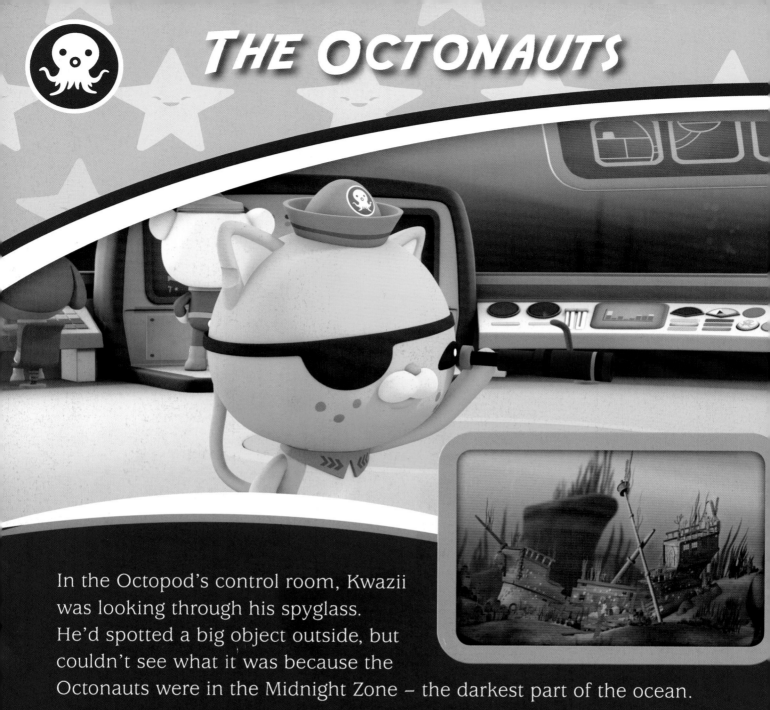

In the Octopod's control room, Kwazii was looking through his spyglass. He'd spotted a big object outside, but couldn't see what it was because the Octonauts were in the Midnight Zone – the darkest part of the ocean.

"Don't worry, Kwazii," said Captain Barnacles, "the Octoscope can see in the dark. Dashi, let's zoom in on what's out there."

An image of a big ship popped up on the monitor.

"Shiver me whiskers!" said Kwazii. "That's the pirate shipwreck of Calico Jack, my grandfather! He had a golden spyglass that should have been passed down to me, but it was lost for ever when the ship sank."

"Kwazii!" bellowed Barnacles. "Sound the Octoalert! Let's investigate!"

The Octonauts gathered in the launch bay.

"Our mission," explained Barnacles, "is to explore the shipwreck and help Kwazii find his grandfather's golden spyglass. Octonauts, let's do this!"

The Octonauts jumped into GUP-A and sped down to the shipwreck.

"Right," said Barnacles when they arrived. "We must be extra careful – this ship is now home to lots of sealife. We mustn't disturb anything!"

"Aye aye, Captain!" said Dashi and Peso.

"Got that Kwazii?" asked Barnacles. "Kwazii— ?"

But Kwazii had disappeared!

Outside in the dark, dark water, Kwazii was swimming towards the ship. When he arrived, he took out his torch.

"I wonder where my golden spyglass is ... **YEOW!**" he cried, as he pricked himself on the spiky sea urchins that were all over the side of the ship.

He carried on – head first into a bunch of seaweed! It was blocking his way but the brave cat wasn't going to let that stop him. He fought his way through

"Me grandfather's treasure chest!" cried Kwazii. "The spyglass ..."

SPLURGE! Before Kwazii could reach it, out popped a big eel that slimed him with bright green slime.

SPLAT!

OCTOFACT:

Sea urchins are found anywhere in the ocean. They eat algae and sea cucumbers.

"Kwazii!" cried Barnacles as he arrived with Dashi and Peso. "What happened?"

"The spyglass is in the chest, but before I could grab it this scurvy blighter slimed me!"

"Get off our property," said the slime eel, "or I'll slime ya again. Three …"

"But I want my spyglass!" growled Kwazii.

"Two …"

"Kwazii, let's go!" cried Peso.

"No! It was my grandfather's and it should be mine!"

"ONE! Let 'em have it!"

SPLURGE! The eel slimed Kwazii, just as he reached for the spyglass. He shot backwards out of the door, covered ears to paw in sticky green slime. *"YEOW!"*

OCTOFACT!
Slime eels can't see, so they squirt slime to protect themselves against predators.

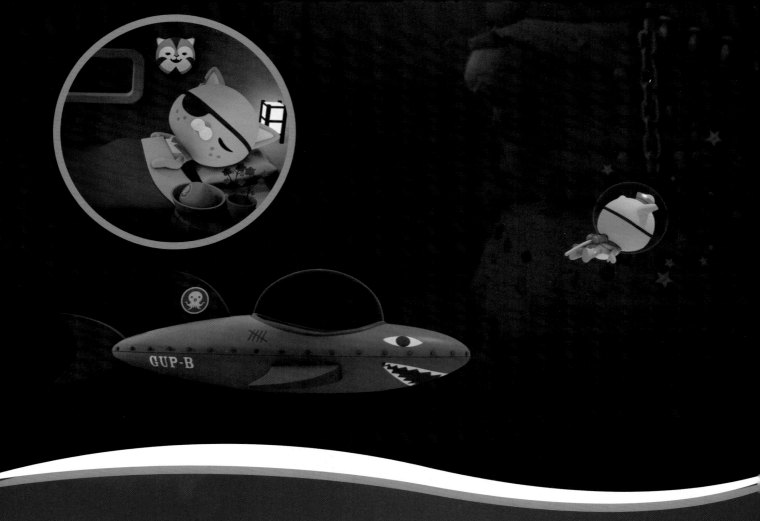

Back on the Octopod, Shellington was researching slime eels.

"Wow, a slime eel can produce a whole bucket of slime *really* quickly! They use their slime for protection," he said. "I can't wait to see one!"

"Hmm, there was a lot of sealife on the ship," said Barnacles. "Seaweed, urchins, slime eels … I'm afraid it's too dangerous to go back."

So Kwazii went off to bed in a bad mood. He still wanted to get his paws on his grandfather's spyglass! He tossed and turned but couldn't sleep, so the daredevil cat tiptoed down the corridor, pounced into the GUP-B and sped out to the pirate ship.

The Gup's engine woke up Barnacles, and he groaned as he realised that Kwazii had gone off on his own to investigate. He jumped out of bed and made an announcement:

"Octonauts, to the launch bay!"

Meanwhile, Kwazii was back in the room with the treasure chest. There were more slime eels now! They were fast asleep and snoring loudly, so Kwazii tiptoed across the floor to the chest. Very slowly, he reached inside. But there was an eel wrapped around the spyglass! Very carefully, Kwazii pulled the spyglass free.

"**YEOW!** I made it!" he whispered. But as he stepped back, he slipped in a puddle of slime, straight into a wooden beam. **CRASH! BANG!** The beam fell and trapped Kwazii's tail.

"Hey, what's all the ruckus!" cried an eel. "So, you're back for more, eh?"

Just then, Peso and Barnacles arrived. The captain saw that Kwazii's tail was trapped.

"We can't move the beam," he said, "but if we can find something wet or slippy, we can put it on your tail and pull you out …"

"I dare you to slime Kwazii!" said Barnacles, cleverly, to the slime eels.

"My pleasure!" said the slime eels' leader, and they shot bucketloads of slime at Kwazii.

SPLURGE! SPLAT!

While Kwazii was dripping with slime, Peso and Barnacles pulled him free.

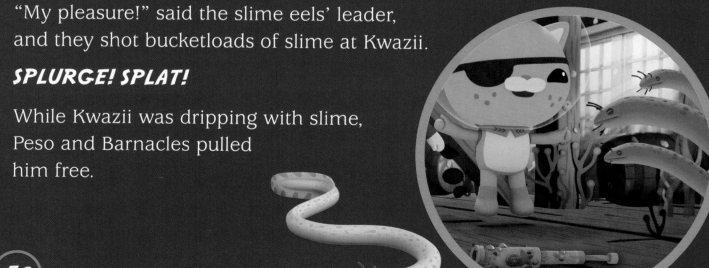

Outside the ship, a slippy, slimy Kwazii couldn't wait to look through his grandfather's golden spyglass.

"**YEOW!** There's lots of animals and plants inside it!" he cried.

"It's become home to many sea creatures," explained Barnacles.

Kwazii sighed. He knew what he had to do. He went back to the slime eels and handed over the golden spyglass.

> **OCTOFACT:**
>
> Most sea creatures need to be underwater to breathe.

"This should have been passed on to me, but now I'm passing it to you," he said. "Take good care of it!"

Later, back on the Octopod, Barnacles told Kwazii, "Well done! Looking out for the creatures in the spyglass was the right thing to do. Never forget that as Octonauts it's our duty to protect *all* sealife!"

THE END

CREATURE REPORT:

Now you've read a story about the slime eel, read this report and learn the facts!

This type of eel lives on the ocean floor.

This eel squirts a thick slime at fish that want to eat it.

It eats worms.

It can't see.

It finds food by smelling and feeling around as it swims along.

THE SLIME FROM THIS EEL IS STICKY AND SLIPPERY.

Now you know all about the slime eel, can you write its name?

slime eel

58

SLIME EEL

This slime eel has been slithering around! Can you follow it's twisty trail of goo with your finger?

In the slime eel story, what does Kwazii find in the pirate's treasure chest? Tick the box next to the right things.

59

Answers on page 68.

MIDNIGHT SPOT

These pictures of Kwazii, Barnacles and Peso looking after a vampire squid look the same but 5 things are different in picture 2. Can you spot them all? Colour in an Octoalert each time you find one.

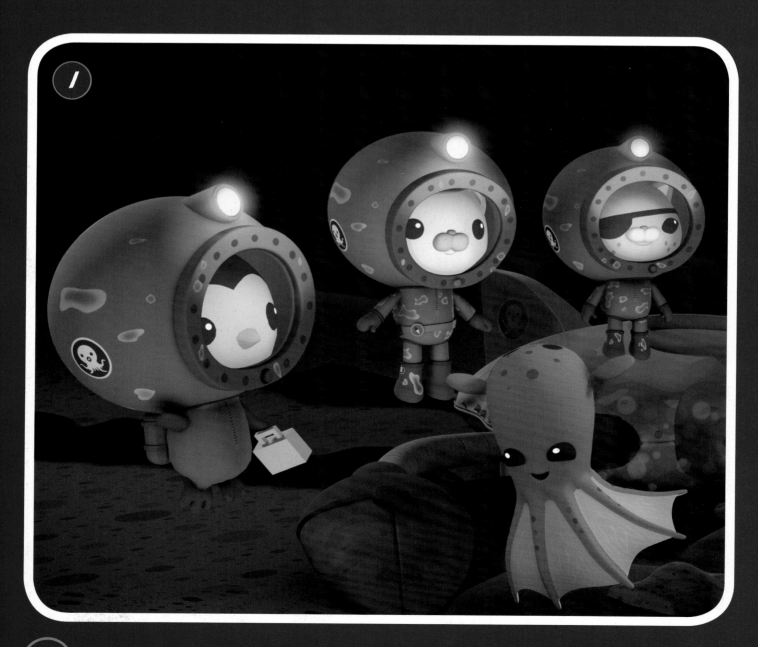

Answers on page 68.

Barnacles is out swimming in his deep-sea diving suit, investigating life in the Midnight Zone.

Can you colour in the creatures around him? What are they called?

What colour is Barnacles' helmet?

How many creatures can you count?

OCTOFACT:
A brittle star can live in all 3 zones.

ON THE LOOKOUT!

Kwazii is trying to spot some slippery slime eels using his grandad's spyglass. Can you help him? You can only go the direction that he is looking in.

START

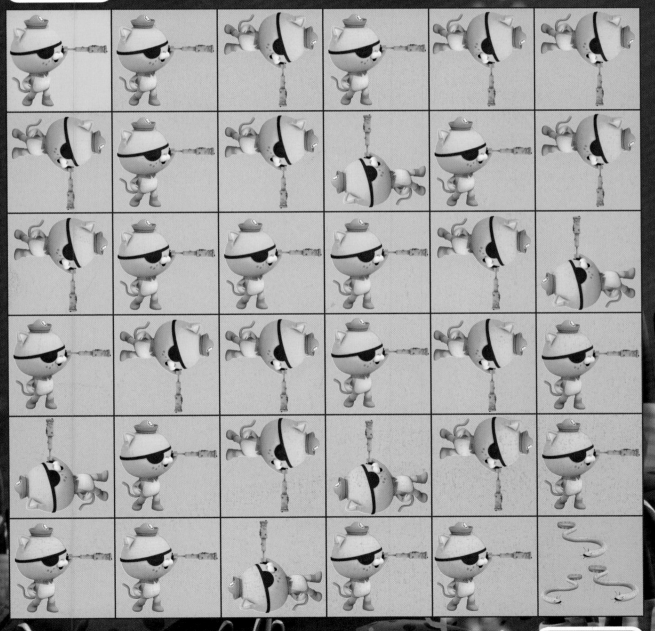

FINISH

Answers on page 68.

MAKE YOUR OWN PESO

Follow the instructions to make a Peso all of your own.

You will need:

- a small cardboard tube
- 1 sheet each of yellow, blue, white and black felt or paper
- a pair of scissors
- a glue stick

1. Cut out all of your pieces. Ask an adult to help with the small bits.

From the yellow cut:

2 feet and a beak

From the blue cut:

a little cross for the hat, a collar and top of the hat

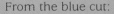

From the black cut:

2 wings, 2 circles for the eyes, a big circle for the head, and a rectangle the size of the cardboard roll for the body

From the white cut:

2 circles for the eyes (smaller than the black ones), a heart shape for the face, a tummy shape and a little circle and boat shape for the hat

2. Put glue all over the cardboard roll. Wrap the black rectangle around the roll and stick the white tummy on top.

3. Stick on the feet, collar and wings.

4. Glue the heart shape, eyes and beak onto the black head. Add the hat on top.

5. Stick the head onto the body and stand him up. Now you've got your very own Peso!

RACE AGAINST TIME!

There's a vampire squid emergency in the Midnight Zone, but the Octopod is in the Sunlight Zone. Kwazii jumps into GUP-B and Peso jumps into GUP-E to see who can zoom down to the Midnight Zone the quickest. The aim of the game is to get there first!

START

1

2. OH NO, A WHALE SHARK IS IN YOUR WAY! GO BACK TO THE START.

13

12. OOPS! YOU BUMP INTO A BLOBFISH! MOVE BACK 1 SPACE.

11

14

15. AN ANGLERFISH LIGHTS YOUR WAY. MOVE FORWARD 1 SPACE.

16

17

18